Acknowledgments

This book is dedicated to all those who are ready to speak their truth and to rid themselves of the pain that comes along with not speaking their truth. My hope is that this poetry journal helps you to find a place to begin to search and open your heart to speak your truth.

May you find love, peace, and hope on your journey to speaking your truth.

Finally, this book would not have been possible without the truth that my patients found the courage to share and to inspire me to write poetry that captured their truth in words.

Thanks for the love and support of my family and friends. To my husband Vern, who has joked that he has been my best patient for the last 24 years. To my son, Vijay, my mother, Brenda, and my sister, Phaetra, for always listening to me planning and processing this project. I love you all dearly. Thanks to my publisher, Courtney Artiste, for her patience with me and my 50 million questions!

Thanks for listening all the times that I, too, have shared my truth!

Blessings to you all.

Natasha

Table of Contents

Coping Skills

Tips to practice self-care/stress management

light a candle *take a bubble bath *pray *talk to a trusted friend *practice daily meditation *close your eyes and take a deep breath *put on some of your favorite music *take a walk *journal *practice mindfulness *seek professional help if needed

Tips to manage anger

identify triggers/source of your anger *count to 10 (or as many as needed to calm down) *take a walk *practice mindfulness *remove yourself from the trigger *use positive self talk *before anger is triggered look at your expectations of what is going on around you- ask yourself will this matter in five days *journal your feelings *practice daily affirmations *seek professional help if needed

Tips to manage anxiety

identify triggers/source of your anxiety *learn about the different forms of meditation and practice daily *participate in some form of distraction (i.e play a game that requires concentration, take a walk, call a friend, read a book) *journal *create a toolbox with things that can help you calm down(this box can include a teabag, daily devotion, picture of someone you love and index cards of your favorite affirmations,) *exercise (always speak with your doctor) *practice daily affirmations *seek professional help if needed

Tips to manage depression

identify people, places, and things that contribute to your depression *create a toolbox that is readily available(can include things that lift your spirit) *pray *practice daily affirmations *practice daily meditation *get the proper amount of sleep *journal *engage in a new hobby *exercise(always speak with your doctor) *seek professional help if needed

Speak your truth about the source and triggers of stress, depression, anxiety, and anger. It is the beginning of your healing!

Find what works for you and stick to it!

Acting

I've gotten pretty good at this
acting as if there is nothing wrong
I have stopped singing what used to be happy songs.

This smile I wear on my face
it's just a cover-up
just a cover-up from all the pain in my heart
I knew you were a mistake right from the start.

I go around pretending that everything is fine
I am ready to start telling the truth
if the truth be told your behavior was totally out of line.

Nothing at all is what it seems
I've gotten pretty good at this acting
just put me on the big stage
because I've acted out a lot of the scenes.

How did I ever let this happen
it wasn't supposed to be this way
I should have followed my heart
it told me if you do this you will have hell to pay.

So that's exactly what happened
it's been a disaster since day one
I want to be relieved from this acting
with you I'm ready to be done.

Maybe I can start by saying no more acting no more pretending
ready to speak my truth
ready for a new start, yes, ready for a new beginning.

It may take me some time to get past this pain
hopefully, I will grow from the experience
I have hope that I will someday soon have joy
yes, great joy and I will be able to dance in the rain.

> *Daily Affirmation:*
>
> *"I no longer have to pretend."*

Talk about a relationship from which you need to be freed.

My Truth

_____

_____

_____

_____

_____

_____

_____

_____

_____

_____

_____

_____

_____

_____

_____

_____

_____

Coping skill I will use today: _____

_____

My Truth

_____

_____

_____

_____

_____

_____

_____

_____

_____

_____

_____

_____

_____

_____

_____

_____

_____

_____

_____

_____

_____

Crashing In

Your love came crashing in
I wonder what I ever did
what could I ever have done
to deserve such a friend.

Your love came crashing in
like a smooth ocean wave
a calm and peaceful wave
a wave that will never end.

Your love came crashing in
please somebody tell me
tell me how did I ever live
before I found you my sweet friend.

Your love came crashing in
like a hot summer day
what a great feeling to have you
to experience you in this way.

Your love came crashing in
like lightning through a fluffy cloud
your love came crashing in
of our friendship I am so proud.

Your love came crashing in like a beautiful sunset
a sunset on a crisp fall day
your love came crashing in
our friendship is here to stay.

Talk about a friendship that you value that brings calmness to your storm.

Daily Affirmation:

"I have the support of my friends."

My Truth

_____
_____
_____
_____
_____
_____
_____
_____
_____
_____
_____
_____
_____
_____
_____
_____
_____
_____

Coping skill I will use today: _____

_____

My Truth

Cry If You Must

Go ahead and let it out
even though you may have such doubt.
Cry if you must, cry if you must,
go ahead and cry if you must.

Go ahead and cry if you must
just let those tears be a sign of trust.
Trust that everything will work out right
trust that you will not give up and lose this fight.

Tears are meant to be shared
to heal us to make us whole
for they come from a place deep within our soul.

Tears are a sign that you are going in the right direction
they speak what our heart can't say.
A total confession
letting our heart lead the way.

Go ahead and let the tears roll down your cheek
don't worry they are not a sign of defeat.
Instead they are just the opposite they are working for your good
tears somehow get misunderstood.

So go ahead and shed those tears
just be thankful that someone hears.
Go ahead and cry if you must
let the tears roll and stop putting up a fuss.

Those tears are precious as silver and gold
they are just another sign that you are brave and bold.
What a wonderful thing that crying can do
go ahead and cry if you must, you have nothing to lose.

Share one thing about which you have been holding back tears.

Daily Affirmation:

"There is power in my tears."

My Truth

_____
_____
_____
_____
_____
_____
_____
_____
_____
_____
_____
_____
_____
_____
_____
_____
_____
_____
_____
_____

Coping skill I will use today: _____

_____

My Truth

_____

_____

_____

_____

_____

_____

_____

_____

_____

_____

_____

_____

_____

_____

_____

_____

_____

_____

_____

_____

_____

_____

Depression

How do I let go of this thing they call depression?
When will it go away?
It feels as if I'm drowning
I'm feeling such oppression.

How do I let go of this thing they call depression?
All of these mixed feelings every day.
It keeps getting harder and harder
just feels like a bad obsession.

How do I let go of this thing called depression?
It's been a really long road.
The journey gets hard sometimes
maybe I'll just start with a little confession.

How do I let go of this thing they call depression?
This thing that seems to rip my heart apart.
How long must this go on
before I learn my lesson?

How do I let go of this thing they call depression?
There must be a way.
There must be a way
somebody please help me
help keep me from going astray.

Share one thing about which you are depressed. List three things you can do to help improve your depression.

Daily Affirmation:

"I am in control of my feelings."

My Truth

_____

_____

_____

_____

_____

_____

_____

_____

_____

_____

_____

_____

_____

_____

_____

_____

_____

_____

_____

Coping skill I will use today: _____

_____

My Truth

Finally

Finally, I have arrived! No more tears, no more fears.
I have arrived, yes! Now I have happy tears.
Finally, I have arrived; it has been a long time coming.
Now I can skip along as a bird to my humming!

Finally, I have arrived. I now have a new perspective on life.
I have arrived, no more loneliness and no more strife.
Finally, I have arrived; my smile is for real.
It has been a long time coming, trying so hard to heal.

Finally, I have arrived, able to feel happiness
I cannot say it has been painless.
Finally, I have arrived, oh, how there used to be so much grief!
Oh, but now there is such a great relief!

Finally, I have arrived! Oh what a great feeling!
I have arrived, thankful that I have done such healing.
Finally, able to laugh, able to smile. I have indeed arrived.
Joy in my heart, now I can thrive!

Finally, yes, finally, I have arrived!

Talk about something you look forward to celebrating.

> *Daily Affirmation:*
>
> *"I have finally arrived."*

My Truth

_____

_____

_____

_____

_____

_____

_____

_____

_____

_____

_____

_____

_____

_____

_____

_____

_____

Coping skill I will use today: _____

_____

My Truth

Fractured but Not Broken

At times it feels as if your heart is broken
so many words unsaid
so many thoughts unspoken.

It feels as if you can't get ahead
taking one step forward and two steps back
full of doom and full of dread.

Then in your spirit something is said
you may be fractured but not broken, just hang on tight
don't give in and don't give up
no, don't give up the fight.

Although the road seems long and lonely
just know that someone cares
just be patient the time is coming
for alone your struggles you do not have to bear.

You have been sad and carrying this load
remember, you may be fractured but not broken
you can make it although it's been a long road.

Yes, you can make it
you will survive
your heart is in a thousand pieces
hold on the day is coming when you will feel alive.

Fractured but not broken
one day you will be whole again
keep your head up
the pain in your heart will soon be spoken.

Talk about something you can do to help improve your mental health.

My Truth

_____
_____
_____
_____
_____
_____
_____
_____
_____
_____
_____
_____
_____
_____
_____
_____
_____
_____
_____

Coping skill I will use today: _____

_____

My Truth

_____

_____

_____

_____

_____

_____

_____

_____

_____

_____

_____

_____

_____

_____

_____

_____

_____

_____

_____

_____

_____

_____

Free

She just wanted to be free
Free to love, free to laugh
She just wanted to be free
Free to find her own path.

She just wanted to be free
Free to speak her own mind
She just wanted to be free
Free to be on her own time.

She just wanted to be free
Free to be who she truly was
She just wanted to be free
Free to be what she was created from above.

She just wanted to be free
Free to feel at peace
She just wanted to be free
Free to receive her increase.

She just wanted to be free
Free to spread her own wings
She just wanted to be free
Free to be able to sing.

She just wanted to be free
Free to love someone new
She just wanted to be free
Free to see from a new point of view.

> *Daily Affirmation:*
>
> *"I embrace a new beginning."*

Talk about one thing that you would like to release in order to feel free. Identify one action step you can take to meet this goal.

My Truth

_____

_____

_____

_____

_____

_____

_____

_____

_____

_____

_____

_____

_____

_____

_____

_____

_____

_____

_____

_____

_____

_____

Coping skill I will use today: _____

_____

My Truth

_____

_____

_____

_____

_____

_____

_____

_____

_____

_____

_____

_____

_____

_____

_____

_____

_____

_____

_____

Here Too Long

Today's a new day, time to move on
to feeling better and to thinking positive
to feeling self-confident and strong.

These feelings of sadness and anxiety have been here too long
time to make a change
time to make a change
a change to where I belong.

Where I belong is a place of contentment
a place of happiness
thankful I have the support of my family
family who were heaven sent.

These feelings of gloom have been here too long
there is no room for you to stay
I am ready for a new beginning
ready for a new day.

I'm ready to see what the world has in store for me
new hope, new challenges
new things awaiting me
I am ready to move on
just you wait and see.

Talk about one thing from which you are ready to move on.

> *Daily Affirmation:*
>
> *"It is okay to move on."*

My Truth

_____
_____
_____
_____
_____
_____
_____
_____
_____
_____
_____
_____
_____
_____
_____
_____
_____
_____
_____
_____

Coping skill I will use today: _____

_____

My Truth

Hope

Today's the day that I have found my hope
able to leave the past behind
no, I will not sit around and just mope.

Hope is keeping a smile on my face
Oh, how I long to be in a different place.

A place of hope, a place of healing
just to be able to share all of my feelings.

I no longer want to be stuck
I have decided deep in my heart is where hope will be tucked.

This newfound hope is keeping a smile on my face
I've decided now is the time to get back in the race.

This hope I've found I'm eager for us to remain friends
I don't plan on giving up, no, my broken heart is on the mend.

I'm hopeful that this is the beginning of a new way of life
newfound hope and much needed joy
yes, a new way of life free of strife.

Hope is the only thing I have left
the only thing on which I can depend
the only thing I feel I have available to help.

I'm excited to see what this newfound hope will bring
on to it will I cleave
hopefully, it will bring new life
taking away some of the sting.

Talk about something for which you are hopeful.

Daily Affirmation:

"Hope is keeping a smile on my face."

My Truth

_____

_____

_____

_____

_____

_____

_____

_____

_____

_____

_____

_____

_____

_____

_____

_____

_____

_____

Coping skill I will use today: _____

_____

My Truth

How Much Longer

How much longer must we stay here if we can't get along,
how much longer of this should we prolong?
Every day is a battle, every day is a struggle
we can't even say one word
without getting into an argument, each of us going unheard.

Why is it so hard, why must it be this way
why can't we just easily say what we have to say?
No matter what I say it seems it's never right
I can't read your mind and say what you might.

What would it take for us just to get along
for each of us to feel that we just belong?
I don't want to continue in this contentious atmosphere
how much longer must we stay here?

It's clear to see that this just isn't meant to be
no ones to blame
not you, no, neither me.
How much longer must we go on
let's just hug and say goodbye
I don't know about you but I'm tired of living this lie.

> *Daily Affirmation:*
>
> *"It is okay to let go."*

It's really unfair of us to keep dragging each other down
I'm willing to do whatever it takes to get rid of this frown.
So if you care for me like you say you do
let me go and I will do the same for you.

Hopefully it won't be much longer before the truth is revealed
maybe then and only then can we start to heal.
Let you be you and me be me
maybe then we both will be free.

Talk about something that you are holding on to that you need to let go.

My Truth

_____

_____

_____

_____

_____

_____

_____

_____

_____

_____

_____

_____

_____

_____

_____

_____

_____

_____

_____

Coping skill I will use today: _____

_____

My Truth

I Don't Know Why

You ask me what's wrong
you want me to explain
I don't know, I can't tell you
from whence cometh the pain.

You want me to tell you what is wrong and why
I don't know, I can't tell you
no, I can't tell you why
the tears are in my eyes.

I can't explain the tears
the sadness and the doubt
all I know is that it is all starting to mount.

Doubt about how to make my next move
to myself only do I have something to prove
not knowing which steps to take
afraid of the decision I will have to make.

> *Daily Affirmation:*
>
> *"I am getting stronger day by day."*

I sit and cry
I don't know why
the tears won't stop
no matter how hard I try.

I can't seem to figure it out
just what to do
to stop the flow of these tears
that have been streaming down for far too many years.

As each day passes by
the tears continue down my cheek
I am desperately trying to find the why
so that this pain can retreat.

Why so much pain
why so many tears
why must I feel this way
what will I ever gain?

List two situations for which you have unexplainable tears.

My Truth

_____

_____

_____

_____

_____

_____

_____

_____

_____

_____

_____

_____

_____

_____

_____

_____

_____

_____

_____

_____

Coping skill I will use today: _____

_____

My Truth

Just for Today

Just for today, let me be me
no false pretending
you get exactly what you see.

Just for today, please give me some space
can't you see this look upon my face?

Just for today, let me say what I want to say
please take ten steps back and let me lead my own way.

Just for today, please don't try to manipulate my thoughts
what's good for you may not be good for me
let me accept my own faults.

Just for today, please don't judge me, let me be what I will be
it may not make sense to you but just wait and you will see.

Just for today, let me be who I want to be
let me live my life so that I can be free.

Just for today, please let me do my own thing
I know you want to help, but I am finding my own dance
my own song to sing.

Just for today, please don't help me
let me see what I can do
I'm sure I'm capable
I have what it takes to get through.

Talk about a situation in which you need to be more assertive.

Daily Affirmation:

"I am capable of leading my own way."

My Truth

_____
_____
_____
_____
_____
_____
_____
_____
_____
_____
_____
_____
_____
_____
_____
_____
_____
_____
_____

Coping skill I will use today: _____

_____

My Truth

Leaving

Walking away is the hardest thing she ever had to do
you gave her no choice
your behavior gave her the blues.

Walking away never seemed like a real choice
she decided it was after you raised your voice.

What good was it for her to stay
fussing and fighting became the subject of most days.

The thought of leaving at first seemed so sad
but the closer it got her heart seemed to be glad.

She never wanted to turn her back on you
what in the world did you ever expect her to do?

Your mood swings became just too much for her to bear
living day by day not knowing how you were going to react
it all seemed just so unfair.

She prayed and prayed for things to change
it seemed no matter what
it was just a losing game.

Leaving is the only option left on the table
she must find the courage to do what must be done
she has to find the place in life where she will be stable.

One thing she knows to be true
this has gone on for way too long
she is ready to start anew.

Talk about something from which you need to walk away.

Daily Affirmation:

"It's okay for me to walk away from people, places, or things that hurt me."

My Truth

_____

_____

_____

_____

_____

_____

_____

_____

_____

_____

_____

_____

_____

_____

_____

_____

_____

_____

_____

_____

Coping skill I will use today: _____

_____

My Truth

Let Me Be Me

Let me be me
please don't try to change who I am
let me be me so I do not get overwhelmed.

Let me be me
please don't tell me how to feel
let me be me and give me some time to heal.

Let me be me and I will let you be you
please do not try to tell me
no, don't tell me what to do.

Let me be me
don't try to change my thoughts
let me be me
with all of my faults.

Let me be me
thank you, but not today
let me be me
please walk the other way.

Let me be me
just the way I am
let me be me
please sir and please ma'am.

Let me be me
to do so as I desire
your anger and control
of them both I am starting to tire.

Let me be me
you are no longer in control
let me be me
I am ready to free my soul.

Let me be me
I am ready to soar high
making my own decisions
so for now this is goodbye.

> *Daily Affirmation:*
>
> *"I am ready to soar high."*

Talk about someone or something that is controlling. Identify one goal to take control of the situation.

My Truth

_____

_____

_____

_____

_____

_____

_____

_____

_____

_____

_____

_____

_____

_____

_____

_____

_____

_____

_____

Coping skill I will use today: _____

_____

My Truth

Missing You

It's been a long time since I've seen you
since I've recognized your face
tell me what is so hard about us
about us both being in the same place?

It's been a long time since I've seen your smile
there are a lot of things about you
that have not been here for a while.

Missing you doing all the fun things you used to do
tell me where has she gone
I wonder if she is somewhere feeling alone?

The frown on your face, the sadness in your eyes
I'm sure everyone knows you're trying to put on a great disguise.
Pretending and acting like everything is fine
the tears streak down your face
give away a much needed sign.

Missing you is the hardest thing I have ever had to do
I'm going to make it my mission to find you
I know she is in there, I know she is somewhere around, I'm going to continue to look for
you until you can be found.

Memories of you burn deep in my heart
I'm going to do my very best to do my part.
To find you to bring you back
to put a smile on your face and happiness in your heart
yes, this time will not be an act.

So until we meet again,
Me

Talk about something you miss about yourself that you would like to work on bringing
back.

My Truth

_____

_____

_____

_____

_____

_____

_____

_____

_____

_____

_____

_____

_____

_____

_____

_____

_____

_____

_____

_____

_____

Coping skill I will use today: _____

_____

My Truth

One Day

One day I will be free
free from all of this anxiety
One day I will be free
free to live, free to be.

One day I will be free
free to laugh, love, and smile
One day I will be free
oh, so free
free just to be me.

One day I will be free
free from of all this anxiety
One day I will be free
free from thoughts that overtake me.

One day I will be free
free to talk without shame
One day I will be free
free to stop taking all the blame.

One day I will be free
free to accept myself as I am
One day I will be free
free from all this anxiety.

One day I will be free
free to speak my truth
free to tell it all.
One day I will be free
free to take down this giant wall.

Share one thing that causes you to feel anxious. List three things you can do to manage this anxiety.

Daily Affirmation:

"I am free of my anxiety."

My Truth

_____

_____

_____

_____

_____

_____

_____

_____

_____

_____

_____

_____

_____

_____

_____

_____

_____

_____

_____

Coping skill I will use today: _____

_____

My Truth

Peace

I need you to stay with me tonight
I need you to not leave
peace I need you to stay with me tonight
to my heart I need you to cleave.

I need you to stay with me tonight, I need to feel you near
peace I need you to stay with me tonight
help me to get rid of this fear.

I need you to stay with me tonight
I see you coming around the corner
just around the bend
peace I need you to stay with me tonight
come quickly and hold my hand.

You came and stayed with me tonight
what a relief it's been
don't leave me, please don't leave me
I need you as my friend.

> *Daily Affirmation:*
>
> *"I deserve peace in my life."*

You came and stayed with me tonight
like the waves you came crashing in
I felt your presence close to me
please don't let this feeling ever end.

You came to stay with me tonight
I'm thankful for this time with you
this peace I'll hold on to
please help me no matter what I am going through.

Talk about something for which you need peace in your life.

My Truth

_____

_____

_____

_____

_____

_____

_____

_____

_____

_____

_____

_____

_____

_____

_____

_____

_____

_____

_____

_____

_____

Coping skill I will use today: _____

_____

My Truth

The Lady Across the Room

The lady across the room said, "Hi, my name is Susie. I'm an alcoholic"
it seem like it was the hardest thing for her to do
but her confession was exactly what I had been going through.

The lady across the room seemed so brave
she told her truth to the crowd
I was so proud that, I, too, told my secret out loud.

You see, I, too, have been drinking
I have not had the courage to say
the last few weeks I have been sinking.

The lady across the room
tears just ran down her face
who would have thought we would both be in the same place.

I can see so much pain as you shared what was deep in your soul
I feel your loneliness
as if you have been left out in the cold.

The lady across the room
she made eye contact with me
I could see it was then that she knew
yes, she knew that I, too, felt free.

The lady across the room
now she walked with a light step
the courage of admitting seems to have added so much pep.

What a relief it has been
to share the secret from down in my heart
the lady across the room and I both are on our way to a new start.

Talk about something that you have not shared that you need to disclose.

Daily Affirmation:

"I am ready to start sharing my truth."

My Truth

_____

_____

_____

_____

_____

_____

_____

_____

_____

_____

_____

_____

_____

_____

_____

_____

_____

_____

Coping skill I will use today: _____

_____

My Truth

The Long Road

It seems as if the road is long
I have nowhere to turn
in the middle of the night
my pillow the tears do burn.

It seems as if the road is long, winding and narrow
it seems as if there is no where to turn around
no directions, no arrows.

It seems as if the road is long
there seems to be no place to rest
please someone tell me
this has got to be a test.

It seems as if the road is long
the signs only point to pain
it seems the weather only forecast rain.

It seems as if the road is long
I'm desperately trying to find a place to get off
going round and round and round and round
apparently I must be lost.

It seems as if the road is long
no signs to tell me where to go
I've traveled far too long
I'm starting to tire traveling to and fro.

It seems as if the road is long
I must have missed my sign
pointing me in the right direction
keeping me inside the yellow line.

It seems as if the road is long
it's nobody's fault but mine
because I must admit
that years ago I saw the signs.

> *Daily Affirmation:*
>
> *"I am being honest about the warning signs."*

Talk about one truth you saw but ignored the signs. What impact has this had on your life?

My Truth

_____

_____

_____

_____

_____

_____

_____

_____

_____

_____

_____

_____

_____

_____

_____

_____

_____

_____

Coping skill I will use today: _____

_____

My Truth

The Past

Sometimes thoughts from the past haunt me like a thief in the night
scaring me,tormenting me
leading me to take flight.

Thoughts of my past seem never ending
like a river that flows on and on
can I ever stop pretending?

I am learning that the past is the past
I must forgive those who hurt me
I must take off this mask.

It's never too late to make peace with my past
it won't be an easy thing to do
but I have to do it at last.

Past I am leaving you
leaving you here where you belong
here in the past
you cannot come along.

You can't come with me
there's no room for you
no room where I'm going
I'm done feeling blue.

I'm ready to move ahead
there's no stopping me now
I'm prepared for whatever comes my way
this is my vow.

Yesterday's gone, tomorrow is not promised
so I leave my past behind
and focus on today
I can handle whatever comes my way.

Talk about one thing from your past that you would like to leave in the past.

Daily Affirmation:

"Today I choose to leave my past behind."

My Truth

_____

_____

_____

_____

_____

_____

_____

_____

_____

_____

_____

_____

_____

_____

_____

_____

_____

_____

Coping skill I will use today: _____

_____

My Truth

The Truth

I can't seem to get you out
I just need to be able to say
what's on my mind
before it goes astray.

The truth seems to be stuck inside
can't seem to get you out
no matter what I have tried.

I must be able to speak the truth
it's keeping me all choked up inside
what else can I do to speak the truth
it's keeping me blocked otherwise.

The pain it causes from being unreleased
the truth they say
will bring me much peace.

The truth you see it must be told
I can't continue to have it locked up
locked up inside and on hold.

You must come out
you must be told
It is the only way
I will not continue to fold.

I am finally ready to speak the truth
a little courage is all I need
hello truth you're ready to be told
so now I will be free indeed.

Talk about one truth that you need to reveal.

Daily Affirmation:

"There is freedom in my truth."

My Truth

_____

_____

_____

_____

_____

_____

_____

_____

_____

_____

_____

_____

_____

_____

_____

_____

_____

_____

_____

_____

_____

Coping skill I will use today: _____

_____

My Truth

What You Said

What you said made me cry
there have been so many things
I have tried to deny.

You spoke about family
who they say is supposed to care
memories from my past
just bring on feelings of despair.

What you said triggers so much pain
your past, my past
resembled two crossing trains.

I thought I had dealt with all these feelings from my past
it seems I was so strong
but what you said
made me realize I was, oh, so wrong.

What you said about your family history
made me reflect on my own family's dysfunctionality.

My mom was not there for me
all I wanted was to have her near
what you said, oh, how it brought back so many feelings of fear.

This was the hardest thing for me to disclose
the pain, it still feels so real
I guess what you said had such a great impact on me
so now I am ready to reveal.

The pain, the hurt, the sadness alike, I am ready to reveal
although very uncomfortable
what you said can now help me to heal.

Talk about how someone's courage encouraged you to tell your truth.

Daily Affirmation:

"I am recovering from my pain."

My Truth

_____

_____

_____

_____

_____

_____

_____

_____

_____

_____

_____

_____

_____

_____

_____

_____

_____

_____

_____

_____

_____

Coping skill I will use today: _____

_____

My Truth

Which One Among Us

Which one among us is hiding behind the pain
too afraid to speak the truth
wondering what from it will you gain?

Which one among us is painting a picture with colors filled with lies
too afraid to speak the truth
to the hurt you feel you are tied?

Which one among us seems to have lost all hope
wondering and wishing if you'll ever find ways to cope?

Which one among us have a heart filled with pain
wondering if you will ever be able to dance in the rain?

Which one among us have a secret that is untold
burning deep inside just waiting to unfold?

Which one among us have hurt inside too hard to explain
knowing that expressing it could just be in vain?

Which one among us is willing to take a chance on letting it all out
willing to take the leap even though you have much doubt?

Which one among us have the courage to be brave
to speak your truth so that your soul can be saved?

List three reasons why you are ready to start telling your truth.

> *Daily Affirmation:*
>
> *"There is power in my truth."*

My Truth

_____
_____
_____
_____
_____
_____
_____
_____
_____
_____
_____
_____
_____
_____
_____
_____
_____
_____
_____
_____
_____

Coping skill I will use today: _____

_____

My Truth

Your Strength

Sitting next to you, I can feel your strength
as you talk about things that have hurt you so deep
the courage it must have taken to tell of your sadness
secrets you no longer have to keep.

Sitting next to you, I can feel your strength
down your cheek you shed a million tears
the pain you shared from all the past years.

Sitting next to you, I can feel your strength
just know you're not alone
so many of us have walked this same road.

Sitting next to you, I can feel your strength
thank you for being so brave
to tell of your sadness
of all the progress you have made.

Sitting next to you, I can feel your strength
to see how far you've come
it encourages me
to know where, I, too, can come from.

Sitting next to you now, I have gained new strength
because of you I can now share
that which has pained me
as I sit next to someone who cares.

Sitting next to you has given me courage
to share my truths from my heart
to tell of the pain that has been hidden
to give me a new beginning and a hopeful start.

Talk about someone from whom you have gained strength and has been a great support for you.

My Truth

_____

_____

_____

_____

_____

_____

_____

_____

_____

_____

_____

_____

_____

_____

_____

_____

_____

_____

_____

_____

_____

Coping skill I will use today: _____

_____

My Truth

Yours

Why are you so angry
this I would like to know
no matter what happens
no matter where you go?

Your anger follows you everywhere
like best friend's just hanging out
do you ever leave it home or is it always in en route?

You seem to take it around like a charm
but what good is it for you
it only seems to be causing harm.

You get upset everywhere you go
always finding fault in things
yes, fault in things over which you have no control.

You want the world to think and behave like you
but people have their own minds
they don't want to be told what to do.

Your anger is yours and nobody wants to share
can't you just control it because it's really hard for others to bear.
It seems you use your anger to control those around you
sooner or later your luck is going to run out
then what will you do?

You walk around as if being angry is the thing to do
what you don't realize is that people try to avoid you.
No one wants to be the object of your anger
it's just too hard to deal
obviously you don't know how it makes them feel.

They would rather avoid dealing with your anger
often times it leads to danger.
So remember your anger is yours
and not many want to share
There is someone to help; there is someone out there who cares.

List five things you can do to manage your anger more appropriately.

My Truth

_____

_____

_____

_____

_____

_____

_____

_____

_____

_____

_____

_____

_____

_____

_____

_____

_____

_____

_____

_____

_____

_____

Coping skill I will use today: _____

_____

My Truth

Journaling My Truth

My Truth

_____

_____

_____

_____

_____

_____

_____

_____

_____

_____

_____

_____

_____

_____

_____

_____

_____

_____

Coping skill I will use today: _____

_____

My Truth

_____
_____
_____
_____
_____
_____
_____
_____
_____
_____
_____
_____
_____
_____
_____
_____
_____

Coping skill I will use today: _____

_____

My Truth

_____

_____

_____

_____

_____

_____

_____

_____

_____

_____

_____

_____

_____

_____

_____

_____

_____

_____

_____

_____

_____

_____

_____

_____

Coping skill I will use today: _____

_____

My Truth

_____

_____

_____

_____

_____

_____

_____

_____

_____

_____

_____

_____

_____

_____

_____

_____

_____

Coping skill I will use today: _____

_____

My Truth

_____

_____

_____

_____

_____

_____

_____

_____

_____

_____

_____

_____

_____

_____

_____

_____

_____

_____

_____

_____

Coping skill I will use today: _____

_____

My Truth

_____

_____

_____

_____

_____

_____

_____

_____

_____

_____

_____

_____

_____

_____

_____

_____

_____

Coping skill I will use today: _____

_____

My Truth

_____

_____

_____

_____

_____

_____

_____

_____

_____

_____

_____

_____

_____

_____

_____

_____

_____

_____

Coping skill I will use today: _____

_____

My Truth

_____
_____
_____
_____
_____
_____
_____
_____
_____
_____
_____
_____
_____
_____
_____
_____
_____
_____
_____
_____

Coping skill I will use today: _____

_____

My Truth

_____

_____

_____

_____

_____

_____

_____

_____

_____

_____

_____

_____

_____

_____

_____

_____

_____

_____

_____

_____

Coping skill I will use today: _____

_____

My Truth

_____

_____

_____

_____

_____

_____

_____

_____

_____

_____

_____

_____

_____

_____

_____

_____

_____

_____

Coping skill I will use today: _____

_____

My Truth

_____

_____

_____

_____

_____

_____

_____

_____

_____

_____

_____

_____

_____

_____

_____

_____

_____

_____

_____

_____

_____

Coping skill I will use today: _____

_____

My Truth

_____

_____

_____

_____

_____

_____

_____

_____

_____

_____

_____

_____

_____

_____

_____

_____

_____

Coping skill I will use today: _____

_____

My Truth

_____

_____

_____

_____

_____

_____

_____

_____

_____

_____

_____

_____

_____

_____

_____

_____

_____

_____

_____

_____

Coping skill I will use today: _____

_____

My Truth

_____

_____

_____

_____

_____

_____

_____

_____

_____

_____

_____

_____

_____

_____

_____

_____

_____

Coping skill I will use today: _____

_____

My Truth

_____

_____

_____

_____

_____

_____

_____

_____

_____

_____

_____

_____

_____

_____

_____

_____

_____

_____

_____

_____

_____

_____

Coping skill I will use today: _____

_____

My Truth

_____

_____

_____

_____

_____

_____

_____

_____

_____

_____

_____

_____

_____

_____

_____

_____

_____

_____

Coping skill I will use today: _____

_____

My Truth

_____

_____

_____

_____

_____

_____

_____

_____

_____

_____

_____

_____

_____

_____

_____

_____

_____

_____

Coping skill I will use today: _____

_____

My Truth

_____

_____

_____

_____

_____

_____

_____

_____

_____

_____

_____

_____

_____

_____

_____

_____

Coping skill I will use today: _____

_____

My Truth

_____

_____

_____

_____

_____

_____

_____

_____

_____

_____

_____

_____

_____

_____

_____

_____

_____

_____

_____

_____

_____

_____

Coping skill I will use today: _____

_____

My Truth

_____

_____

_____

_____

_____

_____

_____

_____

_____

_____

_____

_____

_____

_____

_____

_____

_____

_____

Coping skill I will use today: _____

_____

My Truth

_____

_____

_____

_____

_____

_____

_____

_____

_____

_____

_____

_____

_____

_____

_____

_____

_____

_____

_____

_____

_____

_____

_____

Coping skill I will use today: _____

_____

My Truth

_____

_____

_____

_____

_____

_____

_____

_____

_____

_____

_____

_____

_____

_____

_____

_____

Coping skill I will use today: _____

_____

My Truth

_____

_____

_____

_____

_____

_____

_____

_____

_____

_____

_____

_____

_____

_____

_____

_____

_____

_____

_____

_____

_____

Coping skill I will use today: _____

_____

My Truth

_____

_____

_____

_____

_____

_____

_____

_____

_____

_____

_____

_____

_____

_____

_____

_____

_____

_____

_____

_____

_____

_____

_____

_____

_____

Coping skill I will use today: _____

_____

My Truth

_____

_____

_____

_____

_____

_____

_____

_____

_____

_____

_____

_____

_____

_____

_____

_____

_____

_____

_____

_____

_____

Coping skill I will use today: _____

_____

My Truth

_____
_____
_____
_____
_____
_____
_____
_____
_____
_____
_____
_____
_____
_____
_____
_____
_____
_____

Coping skill I will use today: _____

_____

My Truth

_____
_____
_____
_____
_____
_____
_____
_____
_____
_____
_____
_____
_____
_____
_____
_____
_____
_____
_____
_____
_____
_____

Coping skill I will use today: _____

_____

My Truth

_____

_____

_____

_____

_____

_____

_____

_____

_____

_____

_____

_____

_____

_____

_____

_____

_____

Coping skill I will use today: _____

_____

My Truth

_____

_____

_____

_____

_____

_____

_____

_____

_____

_____

_____

_____

_____

_____

_____

_____

_____

_____

_____

_____

_____

Coping skill I will use today: _____

_____

My Truth

_____

_____

_____

_____

_____

_____

_____

_____

_____

_____

_____

_____

_____

_____

_____

_____

_____

_____

_____

Coping skill I will use today: _____

_____